by Dorothy Spangler

Orlando Austin New York San Diego Toronto London

Visit *The Learning Site!*
www.harcourtschool.com

Introduction

The Ramos family is enjoying a day at the beach. Everyone has a favorite thing to do. Sandra, the oldest, likes to surf. The younger children, Eva and Luis, build a sand castle. They choose a spot far up on the beach, out of the reach of the waves that could ruin it—at least that's what they think. It takes them a long time, but finally, they are finished. The sand castle is almost as tall as Luis!

Eva and Luis go swimming for a while. Then they have lunch. That is when Eva notices something. "Look, Luis!" she says. "The water! It's come all the way up to the sand castle!"

Luis can't believe it. When they built the castle, the water was at least a meter away. Now, the waves are almost touching it!

"How did the water get there?" asks Luis.

"I know how the water got there," says Mrs. Ramos. "The tide must have come in. Quick—let's build a wall around your castle so that it doesn't wash away!"

The sand castle and the tide

What Are Tides?

Tides are the regular rise and fall in the level of the ocean's waters with respect to the land. We talk about tides moving "in" and "out." But what does this mean? Let's start by thinking about the beach that Luis and Eva are on.

When the tide comes in, the waves reach farther and farther up on the shoreline. The water moves toward the sand castle. The level of the ocean appears to be rising. The point at which the ocean is at its highest is called high tide. The tide then starts going out. Eventually, the ocean level appears to stop becoming lower. It is at its lowest point for this cycle. This is called low tide. The height difference between the water levels of high tide and low tide is called the tidal range.

There is a vertical rise and fall of water because of the tides. Sometimes these movements cause water to move horizontally as well. This is called a tidal current. For example, ocean water moves into the shallow waters near the beach as the tide comes in. This is a type of tidal current called a flood current.

Tidal range

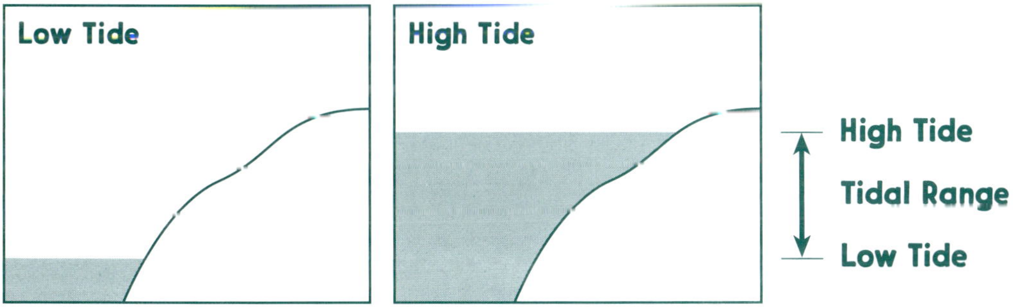

Low Tide

High Tide

High Tide

Tidal Range

Low Tide

What Causes Tides?

People have asked this question since long ago. Some people noticed that the tides seemed to follow the phases of the moon. The largest tidal ranges happen during a new moon and a full moon. The smallest tidal ranges happen during quarter moons. People guessed that there was a connection between the moon and the tides, but it was many years before people figured out just how that connection worked.

In 1687, a scientist named Sir Isaac Newton explained a force called gravity. Gravity is a force of attraction between things, such as two planets or Earth and the moon.

Newton said that two things affected gravity. These things are mass and distance. Newton said that the closer things are to one another and the greater their mass, the greater the gravitational attraction between them.

The tides are based, in part, on gravity. In addition to gravity, there is another major force that works to produce tides. That force is called inertia. Inertia describes the way that moving objects tend to keep moving in a straight line.

How do inertia and gravity work together to produce tides? The moon and Earth's waters are attracted to each other by the force of gravity.

The attraction between Earth's waters and the moon is strongest on the side of Earth that faces the moon. This is because this side is closer to the moon.

On the side of Earth nearest the moon, gravity pulls water toward the moon. The force of inertia works against gravity. It tries to keep the water in place. But gravity is stronger on the near side, so Earth's water is pulled toward the moon.

On the side of Earth farthest from the moon, the force of inertia is stronger than the force of gravity. The water tries to keep moving in a straight line, going away from Earth.

On both sides of Earth, the water "bulges" because of these forces. We call these tidal bulges. How do tidal bulges relate to tides? As Earth rotates, it spins through these two tidal bulges. From the point of view of someone standing on a beach, the largest part of the bulge would appear as high tide.

Tidal bulges are created by the forces of gravity and inertia.

What Else Affects the Tides?

The sun also affects the tides. As with the moon, there is a force of attraction between Earth's waters and the sun. But because the sun is much farther away, its effect on the tides is not as great as that of the moon.

At times, Earth, the moon, and the sun are all in one straight line. When that happens, the force of gravity between the sun and Earth's waters adds to the bulges created by the moon. This produces both extra-high high tides and extra-low low tides. These are called spring tides. "Spring" does not describe the time of year. You can think of it more as the way that the extra-high tides "spring up."

At other times, the sun, Earth, and moon form a right angle. The force of the sun on Earth's waters partly cancels out that of the moon. This results in tides that are moderate, or middle-level. These are known as neap tides.

Spring Tides and Neap Tides

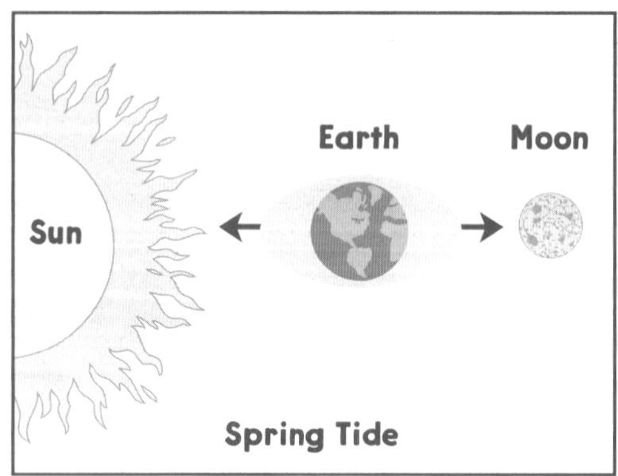

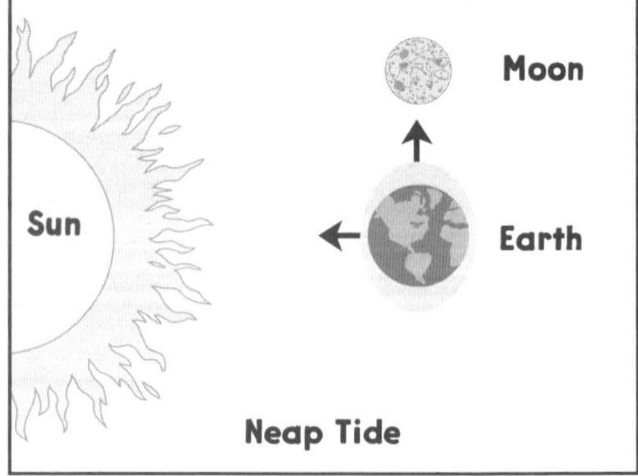

When Do Tides Happen?

Many coastal areas have two high tides and two low tides every lunar day. A lunar day is about 24 hours and 50 minutes. This is how long it takes for a spot on Earth to rotate from an exact point under the moon back to that same point. Each lunar day, Earth rotates through two tidal bulges. This should cause the time between two high tides to be 12 hours and 25 minutes. This is half of the lunar day.

But not all coasts have two high tides and two low tides every lunar day because there are many other factors that affect tides. As a result, three basic tidal patterns exist on Earth: semidiurnal, mixed semidiurnal, and diurnal.

Tidal patterns in North America

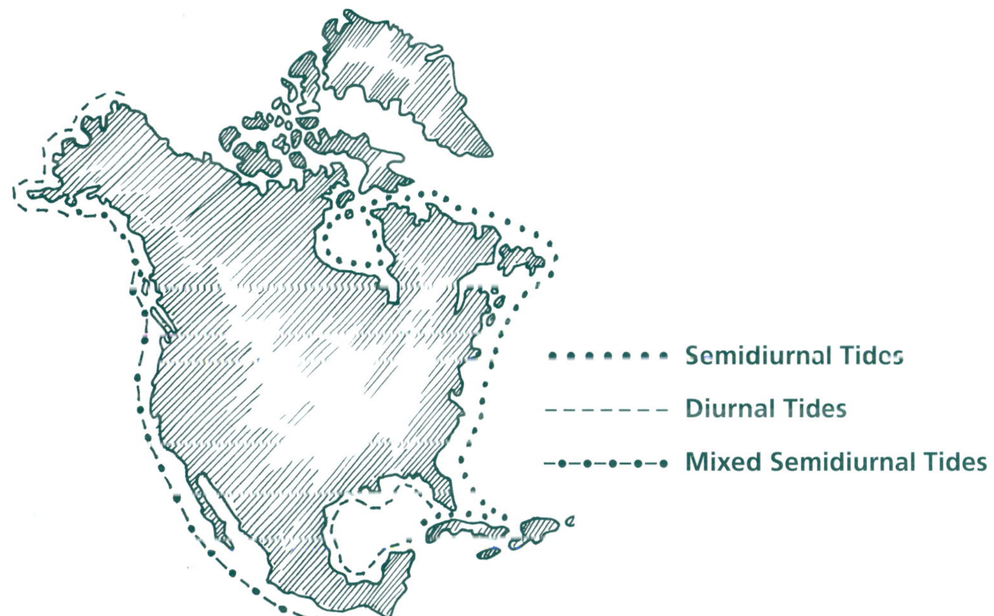

A semidiurnal tide has two high and two low tides in a lunar day. These high and low tides are about the same height. Sometimes a body of water can have high and low tides with different heights during one lunar day. These are called mixed semidiurnal tides. A body of water can also have only one high tide and one low tide in a lunar day. This is a diurnal tide.

How Are Tides Measured?

Eva and Luis "measured" the changing tide just by sight. But people often need more than rough measurements of the tides, so they invented scientific ways of measuring them.

In the past, many scientists measured tides with an instrument called a stilling well. A stilling well was made up of a pipe. It calmed, or stilled, the water inside it.

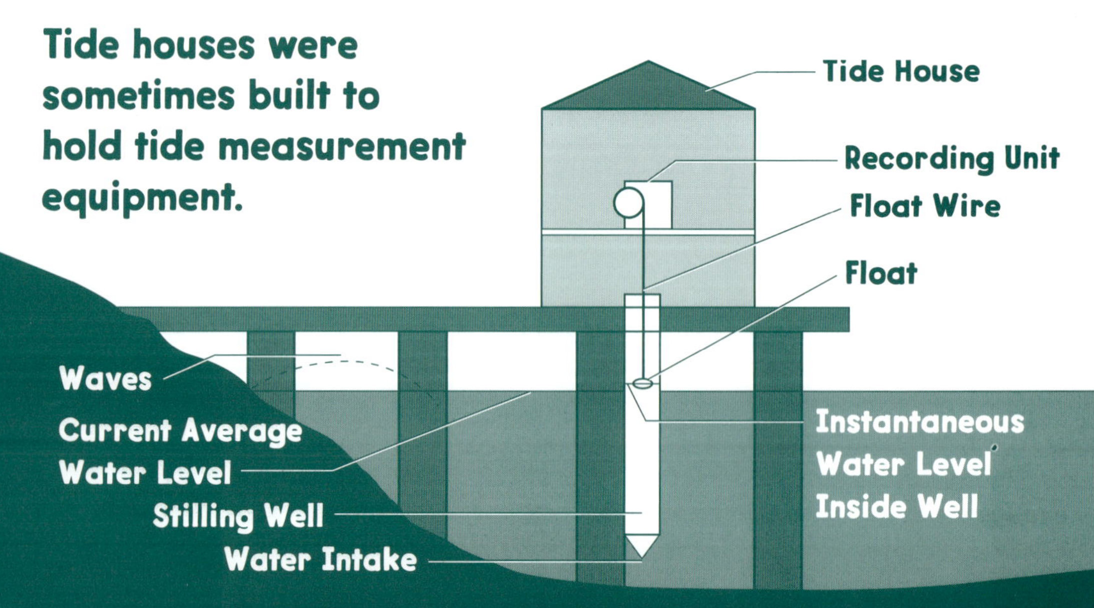

Tide houses were sometimes built to hold tide measurement equipment.

Inside the stilling well, a float hung from a wire. This float measured the water level. It was attached to a recording unit.

Before computers, water level measurements were recorded onto paper charts. Now, those same measurements can be recorded directly by computers.

The way the measurements can be taken has also changed. Today, instead of using a float, scientists use an audio signal, or sound signal, to measure the water level. Inside the well there is a narrow tube called a sounding tube. An audio signal travels down the sounding tube. The signal bounces off the surface of the water and returns. The time it takes for the signal to reflect off the water indicates the water level.

Who Needs to Know About Tides?

We measure tides so that we can describe and predict them. Many people benefit from this information. Those who live or work around the sea often need to know about tides. Scientists want to know about tides so that they can better understand our oceans.

Remember Eva and Luis's older sister, Sandra? She likes to surf. She needs to know about tides.

Surfers like to catch good waves. The tides affect waves. Surfers usually want to know when the tide goes in and out at their favorite beaches. Sandra knows that if she checks the tides, she will find the time of day when the tides help make the best surfing waves.

Sailors on ships also need to know about tides. Think about what happens when the tide goes out. A ship in shallow waters can get stranded on the sand if the captain is not careful.

Sometimes, a captain will have to sail a ship through a shallow water port. This can be very difficult! A port can be busy, like a crowded parking lot. The captain must avoid hitting other ships and must also steer clear of things under the water. If the water levels are rising or falling, the captain needs to know about it.

Anyone who builds things in the water or at the water's edge needs to know about tides. For example, engineers sometimes build docks and bridges. They must make sure that high or low tides will not hurt their projects. So, they study the tides on the place where they are building. They

Busy port at high tide

take all tidal levels into account. A dock that is under water during a spring tide might not be too useful!

People who fish also study the tides and tidal currents. Some types of fish gather in tidal currents. Knowing the tides and the currents helps people catch more fish.

Some scientists also need to know the tides and tidal currents. Knowing how the tides work helps them study the ocean. It also can make it easier to study organisms that depend on the tides.

Of course, knowing about tides can help you when you visit a beach. When the tide goes out, you can look for seashells that the waves have left behind. When the tide comes in, you can make sure your beach towel is in a place that is high and dry.

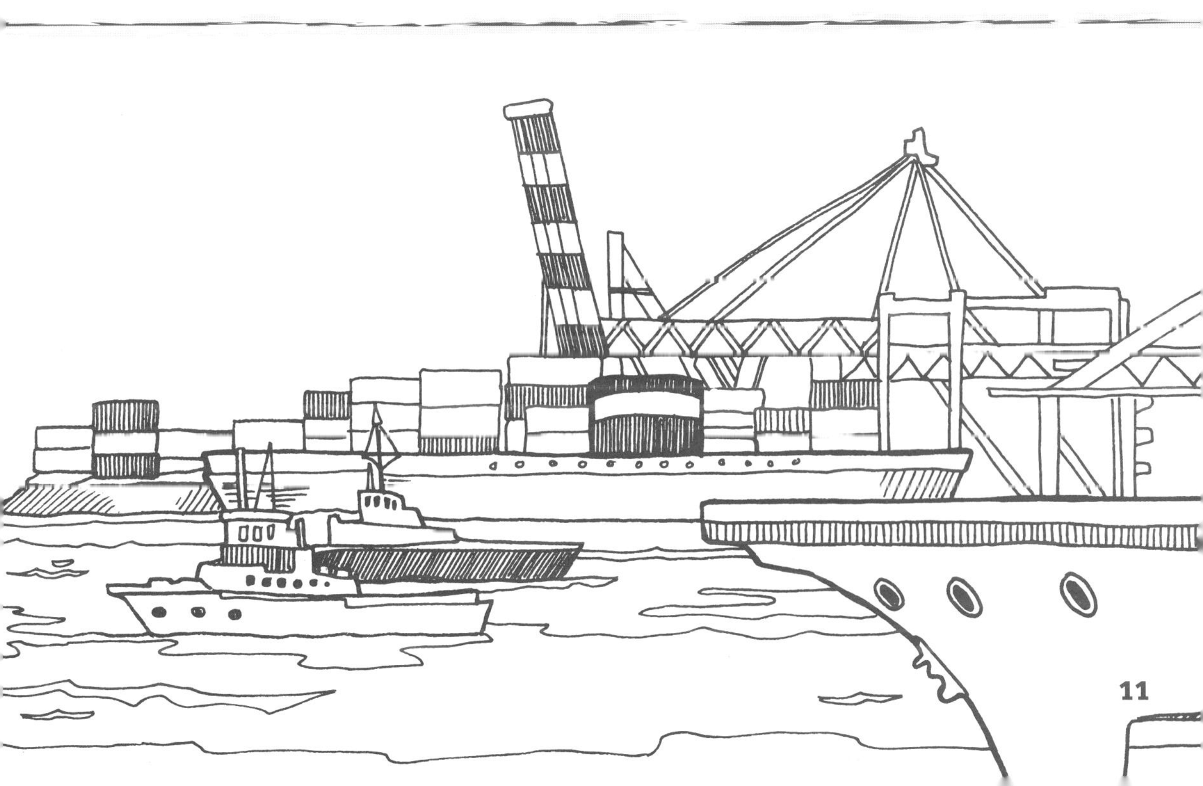

The Moon and the Beach

The moon is not something you often think about at the beach. Usually, you think about the sun. And yet, our beaches and shores are affected by the moon every day. Surfers, people who fish, sailors, and many others depend on the tides.

So the next time you go to the beach, think about the moon. You might even build a sand castle, as Eva and Luis did. But remember to watch out for high tide!